# OUTLIER

# OUTLIER

Kay Sellers

Rev. date: 03/22/2019

**To order additional copies of this book, contact:**
Xlibris
1-888-795-4274
www.Xlibris.com
Orders@Xlibris.com
793915

let us start
with a tempest

.. instead of waiting
for an orchestra to play,
let us simply begin this

# CONTENTS

---

# A B C & D

---

_____

that chaos - the moving van which is delayed. not surprising really – end of may, moving day/weekend – with half the city activated. so inadvertently, we cast off idlers & the lazy. needless to say, the contents of our apartment – couches, chairs, mattresses, refrigerated leftovers, clothes, bath items, & hopes & doubts – recently disarrayed, are now organized for the movers. though some where near the new town, that progressing movers' truck overturns but the populace is there to assist them.

despite the preciousness of our present apartment, our rooms – upper floor terrace, spacious bathing room, closets, two bedrooms(!), a living room, a select kitchen, a den, & dreams & fears – there has been the tedium of months of the fourth-floor walk ups & walk downs. but now, we carry what we can, the not too heavy articles, to the street. most of the residents on the second floor are also leaving & a few on the first floor & the third floor, in anticipation of those arriving or soon to be arrivals. and out of necessity, we eschew zombies & the slow witted.

.. however, if the timing is right, the cleaners we have hired will finish with our new apartment – across town – to appear at the old one later in this afternoon; and this does occur. and so, so finally, the van arrives with a caravan of three others. within the cascades around us, we load the smaller & our movers the larger; so then and there, we do evade somnambulists & the sleepers. nevertheless, in time, we are gone, the moving van & our car towards another part of the city. though somewhere near the new part of the city that successive truck overturns but the citizens are there to help us. in time, we do arrive, consequently this new space, it is broader & on an accessible floor.

on a manageable floor & it is wider, thus this renewed space. yet unavoidably, we discharge ramblers & the undirected. now though, this is moving day/weekend, in the indeterminate city - end of may - inside the indeterminate beginnings.

_____

between us & the next ocean is nothing
        except for the shifting harmonics
that we understand to be the ceaseless wind

        now
because we practice a pattern without pattern
we are followed no less by fanatical measures
        and by intolerant agendas

        now
because we practice an undulating art

———————————

driving west thru wyoming .. we are recalling an old book we found once at an obscure reading room .. perhaps we are only routine passengers in an enthusiastic car .. this very old book, we did find, cited a tale about the first people, they preceded us, who could look clear-sighted into the far expanse & perceive the oncoming next day, another existence .. we are driving with caution, only five miles over the speed limit .. such ancient stories are seldom to be believed .. it does nonetheless create pause, within us, to ponder – as we do look, both of us clear-eyed, into the vast far/ness .. just before we are about to transit into another state .. just before we are about to leave this present time, we inevitably can see what will ensue & what could be destined before us ..

## D /

we have an infrequent knowledge of tulsa .. yet it is here, where we are .. the tulsa of oklahoma .. on a foggy day at the *gilcrease* .. yet where we are, it is here .. the *museum* of the american west .. mists & silver fog are around about anywhere .. a fog is a nonchalant nomadic condensation that has become dispersed .. we are drawn to a not-often understanding of the outdoor gardens .. the osage hills are background .. a fog is a casual roaming succulence that has become disorganized .. we will comment, in a future, about boone grove, senator walk, stuart park, & disseminated statuaries of stone of wood; and the nine gardens, naturally, which are foreground ..

there are four seasons, or technically six, if we would include a pre-spring
& late-summer assignation .. of course, we would know that the planet' orbit is
elliptic not oval & the six, not four, key positions or key locations, in that orbit,
do translate as true seasonal shifts ..

we worship the cyclical .. there is the imprecise almanac, close at hand .. we
worship the earth-bound systems .. the annual farmers' forecast, is close by .. we
drift thru the local environments, as advocates to simple spontaneous living .. we
do possess only an ordinary evolving divinity .. there are the nomadic field-guide,
the book of hours, the honest composition of a compass, the imperfect perfection
of the almanac, the itinerant sketchbook, & our stoic daybooks, near to hand ..

there is a quality of pitch of pulse
to everywhere that we may live ..
a faraway house on a peninsula - lake ontario
an urban domicile, a 2$^{nd}$ floor or a 3$^{rd}$ floor
.

the voice can be our singular music
.. music reverberates in a room

a few hours from now, we shall follow an aerial disturbance,
the parameters of rhythm, in a storm, will attract us,
and the abstract acoustics of storms we will then recognize
    – though we are though, just novices

the world is a room larger than we can possibly construct,
it resounds in the mind,
its music could be our singular voice

G /

————————

in chiapas, palenque mexico, mateo is chasing a man down a street in an unfamiliar part of town. actually, he is chasing two men but only one of them has his backpack. because he is relentless the men become tired and finally the bag is thrown down in disgust. they continue running as mateo retrieves his bag.

now, his new challenge is determining how to find his way back to the bus terminal, since he is quite lost. he reverses his direction and walks cautiously through the dark barrio. then unexpectedly he sees a taxi, or an unmarked taxi, that is waiting, it seems for him, near to a dimly-lit street corner. the driver offers a firmly fixed fee for a return to the distant bus station and mateo accepts the ride after he has perused the interior of the vehicle and he discovers two local women with a small child perched in the back seat. they chime ~ buenas noches ~ in unison, and so mateo confidently climbs into the passenger side front seat. the driver is elderly and grizzled but friendly; he speaks a little english. mateo notices a faint tattoo, still distinctive, on the neck of the driver. the driver grabs mateo's hand and he shakes it enthusiastically.

.

the next day, it is less than 300 miles to guatemala city by bus. but it takes nearly all day, although, luckily the bus experiences only one flat tire. once arriving in guatemala city, he takes to a restaurant on a well-lit busy street and he visits an internet café for an hour. Nearly every evening, during his current journey, he will type a lengthy journal entry to post on his blog. he is curious to find; despite the beauty of the land, the many pleasant people that he has encountered, and the formidable ruins; that he tends to write about pockets of despair, loss, and degradation; this is, in addition, to the hope and the inspiration that is also around him. he is drawn to odd places, to the perilous, and to encounters with the off-beat, and he senses their unique presence and latent history without any foreknowledge. later through supplemental research, in a written narrative form, he will flesh out these observances and sensations for this blog posts.

mateo stays in a reasonably safe and clean hotel that is near to the bus terminal for the night. but the next morning, very early, in the half-light, on the short walk back to the bus terminal, he is accosted by a thug and roughly shoved into a dirty alleyway. there are three grinning men standing behind the burly perpetrator, so mateo automatically and slowly removes his wallet and he opens it. he knows, because of habit, to keep some amount of money, albeit a small amount, always in the wallet. after his money is liberated, he is allowed to leave; he is a little dazed emotionally but otherwise unharmed. he walks rapidly to the station.

later, he is waiting patiently in line, in order to buy bus passage to san salvador. he has one rolling travel bag and one backpack. he has retrieved some amount of extra cash that he had hidden away as backup. presently, there is a tap on his shoulder and when he turns, it is the thug from the alleyway. the man suggests that mateo instead buys a ticket to puerto barrios which is on the gulf coast. mateo refuses. however, a few seconds later he notices a very familiar tattoo on the neck of the thug. it is identical to the taxi driver's tattoo in palenque chiapas. the man gives mateo an enormous bear hug and he says, in rough english, ~ excellent, you recognize me. so here is your money back, from this morning, and now you can buy us both tickets to the coast! ~ .. and although this person is younger, taller, & more brusque than the taxi driver back in chiapas, somehow mateo internally recognizes him as the same identical person, as the elderly hack driver, that he had encountered in mexico.

.

~   i have two questions for you.~ says mateo.
~   are you same person as the taxi driver that i met? ~ mateo continues.
~   and why did you shove me in to that alleyway, this morning? ~

.

the rough man is sitting next to mateo on a bus heading northeast toward the city of puerto barrios which is on the coast in guatemala.

~   yes, i am the same person and i shoved you in order to get your attention.~ he declares.
~   we need to travel together for a while, as you continue your journey.~ he pauses briefly before continuing.
~   just consider me to be a distant acquaintance or a long-lost friend. also you can call me martin or perhaps martina if the need arises. ~ he abruptly stops speaking and he closes his eyes and surprisingly he begins to sleep.

within an hour or so of their destination, the bus grinds to a slow stop. there is apparently engine trouble. mateo's traveling companion encourages him to leave the bus, promising that they will return in time for its departure. they walk, seemingly for a long period of time, through the countryside. they encounter, as they walk, several different small anxious groups of people, with packs, walking northward. it is still daytime and eventually they stop at a lonely site. martin, his newly named traveling companion, fugues into a trance state while mateo elects to become profoundly silent. they both become independently enveloped in a suspended state and they engage in a type of prayer without object. mateo psychologically receives impressions from the past, the present, and what might be possible for the future from this particular site. he will later research this particular location and he will write an entry for his blog.

the bus is just completing repairs when they return. the passengers are restless but everyone settles in as the bus prepares to continue to the coast. eventually, the bus arrives to its destination. upon arrival, his recent traveling companion disappears after mateo departs the bus in puerto barrios in northeast guatemala. mateo passes the night at one of the pricier hotels in town. he eats well, sleeps well, and cleans up meticulously the next morning. he decides compulsively to board a water taxi that transits between puerto barrios and punta gorda, in belize. the spontaneous decision had been birthed by a few innocuous although synchronistic incidents during a brief morning walk in the main plaza area of puerto barrios.

on board the water taxi, mateo cautiously clutches his backpack and one rolling bag. much to his surprise he notices a new traveling companion, with a familiar accompanying tattoo, standing next to the vessel's trip information board. it is a woman and there are between two to four persons standing next to her. on her neck, she has a tattoo of a hand reaching out of a tiny cloud; the hand is holding a chalice. she is a mature woman in good health, obviously martina, who has a backpack and one rolling bag as well. she plants a maternal kiss on mateo's forehead and she then proceeds to unravel a rather large folded paper map of *la américa central.*

———————

shall we thank the breath
that enters us,
leaves us, & allows us
to continue our lives(?)

we see it
this breath,
as it flees,
the elegant exit,
thru an open door
an open aperture
into the porous world

shall we thank the book,
the one in our hand,
that just now,
is showing us
the world(?)

this book, as do other books,
can demonstrate confirmation
of the known world,
what we can prove,
and to some degree
it suggests,
what we cannot prove,
something of the unknown
        of the secretive

J /
_____

shall we give thanks for the falling(?)
or our innocent sinking,
one absentminded morning,
over the edge of our bed ..
because in mid-flight,
before striking the floor,
while in the air above the floor,
while in an ecstatic suspension,
we have had an insight
which is, that insight itself,
if for only a moment,
can also defy gravity

K /

———————————

there is an adjustment, a calibration .. this journey from south nevada to north arizona .. to begin with - henderson, this one city, contains the last of the superficial layers of electronic condensation from that other city, las vegas .. this precedes the outsized materializations, man-made & natural - the hoover dam district, the river colorado ..

we are only commonplace passengers in a motivated car .. but now, how quickly we descend, recalibrate, from a shallow urbanity to the depth of place of the high ground of the arizonas ..

---

on the subject --
any subject of condition --
    keep the intention tightly
    as a silk tie looped & fastened
    about the collared neck
or
    similar to the shoe curved & secured
    around the hosiery the foot

it is that
the binding &
the assurance
of the unbinding ..
a rotational state,
it is *really* that

---

*otra vez a la ola*
*va mi verso* .. pablo neruda

*there is this lake that could walk on two legs ..*
*hay este lago que podía caminar sobre dos piernas ..*

.

dear one:
we know that postcards are old-fashioned .. but we have sent this one any way –
besides, there is the splendid photo on its front-face :: of the lakes in the americas,
this is one of our beloved .. lake tahoe, fresh-watered, is best appreciated by
driving around completely its oval roadway .. this route only becomes perilous
near the bay, that is, a sheer drop on the twin sides of this road, a divine road, &
no guard rails .. nothing between us & *the emerald bay*...

querida:
sabemos que las postales están pasadas de moda .. pero hemos envió éste de
ninguna manera – ademas hay la espléndida foto en su primera plana la cara
:: de los lagos en las américas, este es uno de nuestro amado .. el lago tahoe,
regado fresca, se aprecia mejor por la conducción por completo su carretera óvalo
alrededor .. esta carretera sólo se convierte en peligrosa cerca de la bahía, es decir,
una caída en picado en los lados paralelos de este camino, la ruta divina, y no hay
las cercas de camino .. nada entre nosotros y *la bahía esmeralda* ..

.

dear one:
with caution, at the postal offices, we have asked for an additional stamp, certified,
to insure delivery to the states .. lake nicaragua is an enormous lake in nicaragua ..
there is also the smaller lake managua .. incidentally, *lago de nicaragua*, a fresh-
watered lake, use to be a sea, an ancient one, that is now enclosed by land .. we
are entranced by the strange sea-life here & the watery voices that raise from the
hard waves here ..

querida:
con precaución, en las oficinas postales, le hemos pedido para el sello adicional,
certificado, para facilitar la entrega de los estados .. lago de nicaragua es un enorme
lago en nicaragua .. también está el lago más pequeño managua .. incidentalmente,

---

*lago de nicaragua*, un lago de agua dulce, usar también como un mar, muy antigua, que ahora está encerrado por tierra .. estamos encantados ante la extraña vida marina aquí y las voces llorosos que ese aumento de las olas duros aquí ..

.

dear one:
we have had a difficult time determining when these local postal offices are open here, in *puno de perú*, but we have persevered .. lake titicaca is one of the highest lakes, over 13,000 feet, & fresh-watered, & it straddles two countries, of course, *perú & bolivia* .. the traditional people, the incas, still live, more or less, as they have for centuries .. the lake is considered sacred .. it has numerous islands & the traditional reed boats, sourced from the early gods, that travel between the floating islands ..

querida:
hemos tenido un tiempo difícil determinar cuando las oficinas locales del correos están abiertas aquí, en *puno de perú*, pero hemos perseverado .. lago titicaca es uno de los lagos más altos, más de 13.000 pies, y de agua dulce, y se extiende a ambos lados dos países, por supuesto, *perú y bolivia* .. los pueblos tradicionales, los inkas, aún viven, más o menos, como lo han hecho durante siglos .. el lago es considerado sagrado .. tiene numerosas islas y las embarcaciones tradicionales de caña, desde de los dios ancianos, que viajar entre las islas flotantes ..

---

*este presente, liso como una tabla,*
*fresco, esta hora, este dia,*
*limpio como una copa nueva* .. pablo neruda

to get to downtown, *el centro*, by midday it is possible to take the trolley ..
we ought only to walk a few blocks, four or three, to the nearest station ..
it is clean fast & inexpensive, the trolley .. most people who ride, prefer to stand

para llegar al centro de la ciudad, *el centro*, hacia el mediodía, es posible tomar el trolé ..
sólo debemos caminar unas pocas bloques, cuatro o tres bloques, hasta la estación más cercana ..
es limpia rápido y barato, el trolé... la mayoría de las personas que viajen, prefieren permanecer

once we are there, *en el centro*, we can elect to visit the open market
or we could prefer to the *biblioteca nacional*, especially its adjacent parks ..
first we might retain a lunch meal in the park south of the library .. luckily, we will find a bench

una vez allí, *en el centro*, podemos elegir por visitar el mercado
o podríamos preferir a *la biblioteca nacional*, y en especial su parques cercanos ..
primero podemos comer en el parque sur de la biblioteca .. por suerte, encontraremos un banco

the vendors, near here, have reasonable prices & much improved food ..
we shall retain a recollection, that will continue to flicker, of the best hours of the day ..
this will be a moment that is not like another - in this present time, in this park ..
by chance, we will be fortunate to face the old & wise quarter of the city

los vendedores, cerca de aquí, tienen precios razonables y las comidas mejores ..
vamos a mantener el recuerdo, que siga brillando, de las horas mejores del día ..
este será un momento que no es igual a otro - en el presente en este parque ..
por casualidad, que tengamos suerte para enfrentarse la parte vieja y sabia de la ciudad

---

o /

_____

*cuando cierro un libro*
*que abro la vida .. pablo neruda*

no one knows the true price of a book
without first opening to it ..

nadie conoce el verdadero precio de un libro
sin la primera apertura de la misma ..

there is a ceaseless hunger for words
the speaking of words .. the exploration

hay un hambre incesante de palabras
el hablar de las palabras .. la exploración

books are the containers of worship,
in more than one language,
residing in temples - our libraries

los libros son los contenedores de culto,
en más de un idioma,
que residen en los templos - nuestras bibliotecas

with the plan, in the plans of a city -
there is a place for books

con el plan, en los planes de una ciudad -
hay un lugar para los libros

and who would draw a sky without cloud forms
or an intricate civic site with no thought of books?

y que dibujaría un cielo sin forma una nube
o un intrincado sitio cívico sin pensar en los libros?

_____

and is it not the duty of each new nation
to find its own tongue, its dictionary, its books?

y ¿no es el deber de cada nueva nación
para encontrar su propia lengua, su diccionario, sus libros?

the tonality of books, a quality of voice,
relies on time, place, & intonation

la tonalidad de libros, una calidad de la voz,
se basa en el tiempo, lugar, y entonación

the texture of words, a measure of gravity,
is a matter of context & density

la textura de las palabras, una medida de la gravedad,
es una cuestión de contexto y densidad

and is it not our duty, the all of us,
to embrace the vitality of words,
to open ourselves to it?

y ¿no es nuestro deber, nosotros todos,
para abrazar la vitalidad de las palabras,
abrirnos a las palabras?

———————————————

some days self-select a patina, stone blue clear gray, which is the surface of rain.

.

it has been a place of the past. there was a patina of rain, partly hidden by a tall canopy of trees in a slender park. i had to be sitting on a bench, one in two series of park benches on two facing sides of a broad sidewalk which extended for several & many city blocks. this was near to the broad entry to an urban university. beyond that entry were the edifices of state. it was possible to hear music drifting from one of these .. that one would have been a conservatory.

it must have been a sunday. there were a few of us on or near this campus, on or near a thin park, under an elevated canopy of trees, on a day such as that. and the coffee shop that was adjacent was mostly empty. and i was reading the sunday times, *perhaps* it was the weekend tribune, with mostly an absent mind. and the transients who tended to be often around or consistently about or frequently present, were gone.

at first, you did appear in some unrefined distance, progressing in stages. as i stood to meet you, you did say as you became near to me, ~ we are under now in the tall canopy.~ while how so when as in due course i approached to greet you, i did state, ~ we are couched then in the narrow *narrow* park.~

the scale of living empowers us .. it is the time of the future .. you think -
the old growth forests ought to return .. i think – now the leaves in our trees
should become as pages in books .. consequently, you say - at this time the staff
at the hotel luxx will speak more than three languages .. i say afterwards - my
new friend will soon have new dexterities .. and now/now and, this is an interval
that is forthcoming .. as well as we are empowered by the measure of existence ..
then you feel – there is a sensation that we have yet to know .. i feel besides – it
is essential to understand the inside in order to know the outside .. but now/now
but – yet *yet*, the moon of eupora ought to be the next colony .. but then again,
then i know – that, there will be another type *type* of terrestrial satellite(s) ..

---

there is a category of light here, in this field .. this is a cornfield .. we are walking, in this moment, thru a maze in a field, a cornfield, near north liberty in iowa .. the light moves about because of the wind .. north liberty, by the way - this is not far from iowa city, it is just north of it .. in attendance is an exacting play of light & wind which confounds us .. i do walk to your left & you take to the right .. it is a particular day that is close to november .. how is it that we are alert & attentively walking thru a maze in a field in iowa(?) .. you walk to my left & i take the right .. there is likely more than one probable possible considered approach thru this field with its events .. north liberty, by the way – this is not far from a considerably-sized lake, coralville lake, it is just south of it .. i am taking our lead as you follow .. the panels of interplay, between the light of the sun, the currents of air, & the trails; these indirect tracks; is what stuns us .. you are taking our lead as i follow .. it is actually the last day, that is possible, before november ..

---

we do not know how the radiant clouds follow us -
the vapors in our lives .. this saturated city

.

it is the one large gray voiced polished day
cars stream thru utilitarian bridges
the great barges that live in the sea
are now parked in deep river berths ..

buttons of clouds stain the sky

.

a darkness, is cloud ..

it is a facsimile
a counterfeit
a near similarity
to aboriginal thoughts

.

the clouds in oregon never die
they survive & revive
in a visceral atmospheric
domain of activity

how are these densities of pressure,
quantities of moisture, shifts in air mass,
qualities of temperature &
distributions of light;
and the rare appearances
of sun yellow sun shadows;
how are these, or how is this,
cloud physics?

---

because we love damp dark circumstances,
there is a perfection, for us, in the autumn
of the city & in the winter

myriad scores of soggy leaves clog streets/sidewalks
dark pools of water congregate in low stations ..
there is an elevated absence of fire & heat

we have a notion that the spirit,
that transcendent creature,
is drawn to rainy regions –
the city the river the north the west

we have a theory
that it, that this spirit,
is a panoramic construction
and that it is fascinated
to its earthy complements

U /

———————————

in the background, the event haunts the film

a promising teenager evokes tragedy
another planet has appeared mysteriously in the sky
she, the adolescent, is liable for the deaths of two accidental individuals
throughout the film, that planet gradually approaches earth
a third person, the man, had survived the referenced accident with severities
during the film, it continues, the planet, to approach earth

now as a woman adult, she is released from detentions
the approaching planet especially shadows her
she lives with parents & works as a high school janitor
the planet in the sky, appears to be an image of earth
the woman wants to relate with the accidental survivor, the man

communication is attempted with the new earth-styled planet
while concealing her identity, the woman befriends the man
the new planet & its inhabitants are an echo of this planet
interactions between the woman & the man involve tragedy

in the foreground, the film haunts the viewer

_cinema_ • pina

this is not a documentary but a homage
unconventional choreography, modernistic dance,
and advanced theatre
- an art of enactment

the director fashions the images
dance attributed by a type of walking/moving
the director enables the metaphors
theatre allied by a form of bending/unfolding

sequences, certainly more than several,
        seduce the viewer ..

we are marooned in the deepest part of summer
in the spacious lot, 3 or 4 acres, of our friends,
to the south

it is an outlying vicinity near the wood
near a familiar river

they have dogs & cats & chickens
who travel

in the back lot, their horses are surely dreaming,
while standing upright standing motionless, in their stalls

and here the evening sky ought to cycle thru phases,
although this would probably occur in an undetected & elusive manner

it is just before nightfall & the bugs are lifted up,
from the darken grasslands, into the uneven atmospheres

the low singing of the anonymous machination of irrigation systems
can be heard

at present there is a feeding frenzy .. in flight
are dozens of squeaking birds who are feasting
on the just resurrected uneasy swarms of insects

in the spacious lot, the deepest part of summer,
3 or 4 acres of our friends, to the south,
we are marooned

but we have hence averted our eyes & ears to all of this
because we are instead suddenly focused on, & witnessed to,
the next plot next door

we see & hear two large widely displayed
broad-leafed hardwood trees, if not
a form of local oak tree, before us

and these trees are confident ..
these are the hardy ones that easily dance among the currents
of the uncertain atmospheres

x /

———————

in dreams, we recall repeating outlines of colonnades .. such patterns are, of course, porticos - an outside open attachment of columns .. there is a symmetry to these columns .. colonnades can have, as well, a feature of a form of roof of overhang or covering .. there is a symmetry to our lives .. and usually these formal entryways serve as a transitional space .. our dreams are comparable constructs of these .. transitional space: a portal, a conduit, from there to here ..

---

    we agree that a dream with habitual images of clerestories, rows of eminent very high windows, can initially seem to be too practical .. we do wonder at the height of ceilings .. the commerce of light is everyone' occupation .. we are weighty creatures of stance & volume .. this is architecture at its most restrained .. we are only commonplace creatures of stature & atmosphere .. the arc of assurance, is in a tall window .. the business of light is everybody' concern .. this is a non-obvious source of illumination, the clerestories, into an interior space, into an interior reality .. the arc of illumination, is present within an elevated dream ..

z /

_____

the source of architectural forms will eventually lead us to nature .. natural shapes are a form of organic architecture .. and the architecture of our dreams resembles a river .. that is, it is solid, you can touch it .. and it is fluid, it does flow thru your fingers .. now so, the source of our dreams resembles the beginnings of a river .. it is in an elevated place, these beginnings, that is, unknown to us .. it is in an elemental field, that is outside of us ..

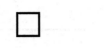

it was the summer when i was a child. this was one of the many midwest cities that did swim in the humid laps of mid-century heat. these were nights we would sleep on the porch. we did tell our stories, the adults first then the children. some said jokes or sang or laughed. we recalled the coppery themes from the far ago. there was my grandmother and my aunt. there was my brother, my sister, and a few cousins. and there was my mother, the terrestrial boundary that did bind us, that cemented us.

so, so soon, so did our voices soften as our eyes fluttered. nearly distant from us were the temporal sounds and sensations we knew of: trucks, buses, passenger cars, and the pleads of emergency vehicles .. and the ripple of trees, the clatter of waiting buildings, the purring of books in the libraries.

it had been the blue evening. and when we finally drifted to sleep, we experienced a splendor that was within and was without. an inarticulate wind did rise. it had been the big blue evening. then at that time, the crescendo songs of crickets of insects deeply descended.

in some neighborhoods, there could have been a distinction of a big house ..
this was at a time as a child .. this was, in truth, a very large house, where you did not
sleep, no beds, also no dining sections, but there was abundant seating .. principally,
in this great house, the people present would then intently have participated to a
preponderance of singing, chanting, & stimulated speaking ..

we were disguised as permeable children .. but then, outside of that, we
ought to have recognized that we had a knowing that was prior to knowledge ..
but then again, outside of that, we might have been especially attentive to our
native inherited normative natural powers which should have been profoundly
pro-creative ..

---

the luminosity, grey green & a few other long thin murky streaks / within & without, the man / at the station / ticket in hand / the surge of passengers, waiting / although the baggage person, with an overloaded cart / with auric tones, yellow & red orange tones / is maneuvering a heavy load / although two teenagers / reclining, concentrating on fierce booklets / have a different burn about them / mostly deep red & a few other lacerating threads of magenta / although outside, beyond the rectangular platform / waves of brown, yellow crisp / this does surround two engineers gazing up among in to inside a huge compartment of motors / although a choral of women / orange purple & a small number of extra extended slender foggy slender strands of mint green / they do handle sheets of a notated manuscript / at the station / although *although* someone in handcuffs / with a creamy charcoal aura / that someone who is guided laboriously by guards / and thru waiting passengers, & the surge ..

kansas city has expanded far these days .. from the airport, north kansas city in missouri, make your way west .. nw 136<sup>th</sup> street; after that humphrey road, after that west again on state road '45' .. you believe it is not thursday .. there are some open areas here to the river .. fields, some fields of wheat perhaps .. you know it is thursday .. stay west, you must connect with the '92' in order to cross the river, the missouri river – north/south flow .. this is a high bridge here because of the bluffs here .. your mind is a closed system .. in leavenworth & lansing, take the state road '7' south .. there are seven facilities of correction here .. your mind is an open system .. you will stop to visit a friend, from collegiate days .. you do not know what anyone thinks .. you will stop for an hour .. she lives in leavenworth, near st. mary's, usm .. you know what everyone is thinking .. this is the kansas side of kansas city .. you are the traveler, from the northwest of the metro to then the southwest of the metro .. you are traveling south .. stay south .. after crossing the river, the kansas river – east/west flow .. you do have fears .. this is where it gets tricky .. the juncture of '7' & '10', take the '10' back east .. you are without fear .. the '10' merges with interstate '435' .. eventually do exit south on state road '69' .. and then there is again southwest kansas city to traverse .. followed by a series of alternating serene open serene areas, some fields farm fields, the occasional village picturesque village .. you are never happy .. but most importantly reconnect with the interstate once more, the '44' this time .. stay south or southwest all the way to tulsa .. you are always happy .. this is the destination .. to oklahoma, namely, to tulsa .. that is your destination ..

the strict winds on the columbia river come from the circulatory exchanges of the pacific .. and this river, the columbia, dividing two states - the washington the oregon - is a river of gusts .. these gusts are the life breaths of this region .. which does quite correspond to the breaths of a city, which is, also likely a result of, or due to, or attributable to, the mass manifestations of the individual circulatory systems within its populace .. the human multitudes - the ordinary breaths of the people, the people ..

the plan of nebraska reveals very little .. the map is starkly drawn .. although it is not the same as an actual experience of nebraska .. for instance, we could take the prime interstate west, that is, interstate 80 westbound .. our automobile does self-select the navigation .. the interstate meanders but there is a category of logic .. we travel on, we drive on, utilizing little more than invigorated air .. the speed limit here seems to be unlimited .. obviously, we have given up on food on drink .. and then, beyond the city of lincoln & the city of lexington, the trajectory of the road itself here, seems to be unlimited ..

there is this sole true cold true clear music -
this is one of the stages

another stage -
the battalions of
ionized bits
of sentience,
these are the
armed forces
of a fleeting
sensational
narrative

inside the mind, the world outside,
may appear a welcome incomprehensibility -
the beauty of divergent worlds ..

so we walk outside,
    it is simple ..
a few unvoiced mountains & a tree
- actually, a perfected tree -
which conceals a form of stratified hallway
- a type of corridor of layers

# OUTLIER

---

an outlier is an observation
that is beyond all other observations

probably the world is not a holograph ..
likely our desires help to create it
-- this manufacture of a real & replete world

and the city that we live in
is a fingerprint
identifying that world

this recess, in the cloud-like room, is a perfect cavity for a large wooden chamber .. there are steep windows aside but the cabinet will be focal .. this will be in our room, among our rooms, within a house that is our home .. we will have other small serviceable simpler requirements in mind but the cabinet, it will stand as tall, as alike a wardrobe, a portable locker, or a repository .. in this home that is a house with the rooms in which resides the stratospheric room that contains the cabinet ..

---

a single file procession
among the hulks of aircraft

we abandon the terminal for the tarmac,
a movable stairway awaits
and we will surmount it ..
vigorous propellers will roar to life,
a long promised runway awaits us

we shall have a curiosity that is just beginning ..
mountainous skylines are in a distance
and we are going to climb them ..

large engines do yet deploy
in far-off continents

---

indivisible atmospheres .. there is something about islands .. and at the same time, the identical time signatures occurring most simultaneously, although in distinct yet fabricated zones .. such a territory of land is one that is completely surrounded completely by water .. time is an island in an atmosphere with no apparent boundaries .. these atmospheres - tethered in naval hues .. the sound of a passage of time is the noise of the sea around an island .. different islands of time are part of atmospheres that are united ..

---

the house, this house, has dormers .. accordingly, we are apt to consider a new way of seeing .. a dormer is a vertical extension in a roofline allowing for sky & imagery, as such, it is an elegant protrusion beyond the pitch of a roof .. we are third-storied individuals, subsisting in a loft-like existence .. furthermore, we are encouraged to imagine a different form of perceiving .. we are as these upper rooms, relating in a symmetrical fashion .. a dormer, as a type of gable, is a structure, with perfect sloping on two sides, which frames a triangular zone .. we strive to be elevated people, surrounded on three sides by atmosphere & representation ..

---

we find an old edition, on the motion of planets, in a literary place .. most planetary objects move in a primary or prograde direction around the sun .. we walk clockwise in orbits about the center of the city .. but still nonetheless of course, celestial objects & satellites can move counter or in a retrograde rotation against their principal direct pathway .. on occasion, we are drawn, as are others, back again thru the city .. retrograde or retrogressive celestial behavior, either temporary or long-term, is not eccentric, rather it is another type of, or a differing form of, trajectory .. a few times a cycle, we behave differently, and we may move retroactively thru the city ..

---

    into the scene, the camera man, actually a camera woman, angles resourcefully up for the cinematic shot .. a person moves an object .. a person, another person, re-examines a chair .. this is all, a sweep of compelling modulation .. makeup or a touch-up is applied to the actor, the main protagonist, actually an actress not an actor, by the make-up artist, this time a man .. it is all, an arc of potent inflection .. someone readjusts the lighting .. and someone, another someone, places & waits to enter into the scene ..

_____

industrial strength plastics/tenting,
or heavyweight canvas, or tarping/tarpaulins
wrap the enormous buildings, that are under construction,
                    as a preserve against the elements ..
this is art .. a blowing/flowing art that one could chance upon in dreams ..

and those massive attachments of skeletal intricate scaffolding(?)
this is sculpture, that is, an expressionistic exo-sculpture
      which could resembles assemblages
that we might encounter in imagination ..

you & i can tend towards dissent, just to be clear, in the most pedestrian fashion, these days .. mostly this is accomplished by leaving postcards addressed to no one in particular, or to everyone specifically .. cards containing defiant musical notations & disobedient harmonic transcriptions .. these postal notes are left in well-known corners within anonymous public spaces ..

we are ambitious escapists .. not unlike bored mezzo-sopranos who secretly improvise problematic sections of a tightly constructed operatic production .. we are as elatedly adrift as awkward sections of music, newly liberated from its composer ..

those charming streets
that you tend to write about
in postcards to intimates back home,
cards sent as you travel in latin america,
are streets happened upon by accident

las encantadoras calles
que tienden a escribir sobre
en postales a íntimos de vuelta a casa,
como usted viaja a américa latina,
sots son calles tropezamos por accidente

and wanting to avoid ob/noxious gyspys,
those ones who stalk the magnificent boulevards;
broad streets where presidents may speak
or where diplomats might stopover;
we are allowed, & well-off too,
to slip into a concealed lane
that is cobbled & pleasantly situated

y querer evitar nocivos gyspys,
quienes acosan magníficas avenidas;
presidentes hablan alla
o donde los diplomáticos podrían hacer escala;
se nos permite, y acomodada también,
caer en una calle oculta
que es decir empedradas y muy bien situado

an aperture into a street
a ratio of windows & balconies
a marriage of the natural & the manufactured
on a not common-placed somewhat horizontal street

una abertura en una calle
una relación de ventanas y balcones
una unión de los naturales y manufacturados
en una calle algún tanto horizontal no común

indigo tones seep from the radio .. the city's all-jazz station plays brazilian singer, caetano veloso, on a dripping morning .. we long for the sweet sadness of former rains .. the expression that one can declare about these tenors of radio music, we recall, in portuguese is *saudade*, a fateful nostalgia, and in spanish it is referred to as *duende*, a soulful nostalgia .. sadly, the rains of yesterday are all of what we can recall .. in english, there is no one sole singular precise particular sole word about it but the sentiment exists nonetheless .. our closest american terminology is probably bittersweet nostalgia .. in an older world we recollect the rains, sadden & burnished .. and as for that discoursed word, from these aforementioned languages, which is, of course, the word nostalgia, as in, and that is, the longing for a former embodiment of contentment in a person, a period, or a place ..

we have a sketch of la paz,
in bolivia, in our minds,
as an elevation
of geometric projection ..
the city near 12,000 feet,
below the towers of the andes,
situated in a bowl on the high plateau

we know quito,
in ecuador, thru our emotional temperature,
as a vertical distance
between two points ..
the city is at 9300 feet,
the andes in majestic stances,
discretely concealing its active stratovolcano

and cusco now, in peru,
the contours are a part of us,
it is a declaration
of loftiness & aloofness..
the city sets at slightly more than 11,000 feet,
the andes shadowed in sepia balminess
extruding over a river *river* valley

the largest metropolitan area in the republic of chile is santiago, or greater santiago[1], at 7 million inhabitants, it is situated in the interior of this slender country at the foot of the andes.

el área metropolitana más grande de la república de chile es santiago, o gran santiago[2], a los 7 millones de habitantes, se encuentra en el interior de este país delgado, al pie de los andes

the 2nd largest statistical metropolitan region is valparaíso, at nearly a population of 1 million, on the country's coast. valparaíso y viña del mar is often referred to as the twin cities on the chilean coast although technically greater valparaíso[3] is comprised of five principal municipal cities.

la segunda mayor región metropolitana estadística es valparaíso, en cerca de una población de 1 millón, en la costa del pacífico. valparaíso y viña del mar refiere a menudo como las ciudades gemelas de la costa chilena aunque técnicamente gran valparaíso[4] se compone de cinco principales ciudades municipales.

it can be further noted: valparaíso[5] is a major seaport, political, and educational center whereas viña del mar[6] is known as a destination for resorts, malls, & entertainment. Naturally, another dynamic of this coastal region, is the presence of a wide large sea, an ocean, the pacific.

se puede observar además: valparaíso[7] es un puerto importante, política, y un centro educativo mientras que viña del mar[8] es conocido como un destino para los balnearios, centros comerciales, y entretenimiento. naturalmente, otra dinámica de esta región costera, es la presencia de un gran ancho mar, un océano, el pacífico.

---

[1] it is advantageous to know that the nation's capital occurs here
[2] it is advantageous to know that the nation's congress exists here
[3] es conveniente saber que se produce la capital del país aquí
[4] es conveniente saber que se existe el congreso de la nación aquí
[5] it is best to wander the idiosyncratic maze of the historic hillside streets there
[6] it is best to meander the placid undulation of the contemporary coast-side beaches there
[7] lo mejor es pasear por el laberinto idiosincrásica de las calles históricas de la ladera alla
[8] lo mejor es explorar la ondulación plácida de las playas del lado de la costa modernas alla

———————

hola, mina / i guess we will leave you a rather lengthy voice recording since you are not answering your phone / (*cough*) we are stumbling about the upscale upward streets of bellavista in quito, with 25 minutes to kill before the opening of el museo de guayasamín / we love his haunting unadorned primal work / the museum will open at 10.00 am / (*car backfires*) pardon, the noisy background / everywhere there are cars & buses, quite a distraction, but yet we are truly riveted by the attractive residential streets, near the museum / we suppose this, this automotive activity, is in advance of the opening of the museum / moving on / there is an orgy of plant life overcrowding the streets, as well as, an overcast of an olive-tinted sky / a choppy wind ventilates these streets / and there is a gauzy flotilla of seeds, tiny flowers, & cottony strands gliding airborne among the streets (*phone beeps*) / and apologies about my beeping phone .. but no worries mina, we are going to ignore that incoming call, whoever it is, they can leave a message, because we need to complete this message / (*phone slips from hand*) oops! are you still there? / that was a close one because I nearly dropped the phone on the hard sidewalk but thankfully my reflexes kicked in / anyway, we are arrested, that is visually, in particular, by these certain bushes, with long narrow thick green leaves, that feature an outgrowth of some type of bell-flower / you have a minor in botany, yes? / (*dogs bark*) and so before we hang up, a queue is forming now in front of the museum as we speak, can you get back to us about this? / I am sure you could identify these flowers / in brief, they are flared cup-shaped undulating cones of red/white, or blue/white, or yellow/white, or other variants of coloration, which are smooth & waxy & honest to the touch / (*click*) oh yes, we will send a photo / besos, guapa ..

———————————

hola mina / please forgive yet another long recorded voice mail but lately you have not deemed to pick up the phone when we have called / (*voices in the background*) so, these last days of february have been a scene but in a good way / (*many loutish automobiles passing by*) these are days we have spent under a spell of halcyon splendor as we bounce between the colonial aspects of old town & the modernity of new town in quito / and we have discovered that one of our favorite vecindades or neighborhoods is la floresta, a college & university induced area / católica universidad is located there, for instance / and this neighborhood features multitudes of students and professors, restaurants/bars, lots of restored old buildings, and a fabulous overlook section which presents a drop-dead vista of one of the massive valleys below the city / (*my partner has a coughing fit .. a short though violent one*) sorry about that, my partner is having some sort of respiratory episode / now back to our little history / unfortunately everything changed two days ago / as it were, we were standing innocently in front of a little wonderfully restored gallery, near a technical college, when we were assaulted by several angry men / ok, perhaps assaulted is a bit of an overstatement since what really happened was a pelting by about a dozen water-laden balloons & in truth it was only the actions of two gleeful men / (*i have a coughing fit .. equally short though a violent one*) i wonder if coughing is contagious / to continue / the proprietor of the gallery explained that water attacks were common & will increase in frequency-voracity the closer the days unfold towards the start of lent / as a matter of fact, we have already started to notice more random liquid episodes occurring on the streets / we believe the first day of lent, will occur soon, around the 10th of this month & then these attacks will stop / what a scene but not in a good way / chao, guapa ..

———

---

hola mina / we have stopped in, for a few minutes, at a tucked-away internet café (*the partner gets up & searches about for a restroom*) / it is also a restaurant, bar, & a curious bookstore, all in one (*takes a sip of water*) / we are e-mailing you with a day-story, from today, about the schizophrenic reality of latin america (*low hum of the background aural noise from other patrons*) / we had spent, this morning, a perfectly charming day, downtown at the open market in parque el ejido / as you may know, positioned near one of the entries into the popular park is the famous archway, arco de la circasiana, and situated nearby within the park itself is literally hundreds of booths of local arts & crafts (*orders a café con leche from one of the attendants*) / beyond the booths are many areas for fútbol and voleibol (*we use the terms, in english – soccer & volleyball*) / and troops of young children in smart uniforms march thru these parklands / we imagined that we were interested onlookers near the edges of these events .. merely watching / (*coffee arrives with a free sample of a torta that the kitchen is experimenting with*) / it has been a rare rainless day in quito & after the park we walked to a little restaurant in the youthful la mariscal district / and yes, we are aware of the advisory for caution, after dark, in this area, but we enjoyed lunch there in the broad daylight / (*the partner returns after a restroom hiatus*) / anyway, arriving back to new town, quito moderno, just as soon as we departed the trolley, near the stadium, our eyes begin to water / we were in the midst of crowds from the aftermath of a soccer match / the mood of the masses was an drunken ugly one / the police were shouting into megaphones / apparently a cloud of teargas floated thru the air / we speculated that we were engaged observers at the edges of things .. simply observing .. / hasta pronto, guapa ..

---

burgeoning foliage lines the street, outside our factual hotel, in a city of colonial radiance; this is sucre bolivia; and the street, or this street, leads to the bodega where we will have our *café y postres de desayuno* this soggy morning ..

speaking of our hotel, the hot water, in the shower, dissipates after two & a half minutes, so we shower together, for practicality ..

regarding the street, there is a haphazard construction zone that exists thru-out the length of this thoroughfare roadway passage, and we walk tightly, dodging unguarded holes in the concrete, arm in arm, for security ..

naturally, the bodega is brimming, when we arrive, with animated people, but then luckily we find that we can sequester ourselves in a free corner niche in the rear of the establishment, coffee & pastries atop a tall skinny half-circle of a counter, & we stand face to face, for economy ..

---

and her place would have a pool .. but it would be in the capital of her nation, santiago de chile .. and this pool, rimmed by flat-faced stone, would be buried flush into the green flesh of the earth .. but there would be an inclusion of some form of some controlled mechanism for controlled heating .. and this pool would be guarded by stately vestments of italian cypresses, the slim mediterranean trees, that surely would be securely matured .. but ideally then there would be her daily swim - nothing would divert her .. and neither the condemnation of the autumn winds nor of the winter rains would deter her ..

we smell of dark liquid .. coffee, a strong french roast .. a java room bathed in an auburn light ..

•

on the jazz radio, astor piazzolla - traffic on the interstate dances spherical & slowly .. the rains do a tango about the atmospheres ..

•

The twisty illogic of the streets, height upon height, in valparaíso .. & the ancient hill bound rails .. these are, for us, the elevated joys, the pleasures ..

•

we walked in a upward ecliptic pattern upon el cerro san cristóbal to eventually past the observatory & towards the statuary & the sanctuary on the summit .. in far south, south america .. on one national & religious holiday in winter .. on one bright july day in cold winter ..

•

radiant neoclassical & historical styles materialize above / portugal, in porto / we try to mitigate our veneration with our own only impractical postures / porto, in portugal ..

•

an uncertain sunset .. probably on an oceanic road, a latin fog – conceivably near to buenos aires ..

---

we smell of flat white liquid .. coffee with an equal part, warm milk .. a java room washed in a blonde light ..

•

in sinclair in wyoming, we are offered two towns .. a refinery commune, with unconfined intricacies of steel piping, mobile metallic cranes, & towers .. and another town, just a little ways west .. a company town - housing, schools, the trees ..

•

the last day here, we spent visiting our favorite locations .. maybe it was the second to last day(?) .. no cameras or phones, only the apparatus of our five senses ..

•

the eastside esplanade near to employed boats, employed bridges, the river .. and so this broad flowing walkway which is adjacent, as well, to public art, public trees, the fencing ..

•

the singer / the voice / so unique as to be / either coldly ignored or addictively devoured / & so you have self-selected to adore her / & so you have chosen to admire her nuanced song ..

•

shall we make a music(?) .. that intangible wedge of base harmonics & melodic tension .. & shall we yet then offer it, this music, with our so lenient & so eager hands(?) ..

---

several years ago, she was fortunate. she had a house with a friend. it was a 3-storey situation on a road leaning into the mountains. on sundays, in the noiselessness of the morning, as a summer light had just begun to crease the sky, armed with a small pack, she sprinted to her car.

there was the seen and the unseen. and on the route into the mountains there were details of flowing brooks, stone rock pillars, flowing groves, stone rock columns, serpentine trails, depressions of terrain, sudden meadows, and heavy stubborn brush just beyond the road's edges. and sounds as in the movement of animals and the rustling of trees were part of this. the delicious mystery was the curiosity about the unknown elements that were present but just beyond the parameters of recognition.

out of habit, she would eventually stop at a parking area that was mostly deserted that time of early morning and especially so, if it had been during a non-ski season time of year. the parking of the car, the fitting of the backpack, and the walking to the trailhead happened. on one particular trail, norski trail, which was favored, it was this trail which had a distinctive feature of a type of a layout, or design, of a series of branching loops. these loops were created to lead one back eventually to the beginning of the trailhead.

aside from the obvious visual richness, what drew one's attention, in the deepness, were bird calls from undetected birds, the wind that rose in the trees invisibly, and her frame, without any conscious effort, imperceptibly moving within the landscape. there was what she saw and what she did not see. all of this was before the hidden sun was just risen in the forest. every element, around her, sensed it, this rising, before she did.

feb 15<sup>th</sup>

.. thought this day would never end, at least, at the diner. Obviously, we are happy, our staff is happy, at the continued influx of regular customers & the new ones as well.

the day started as it usually does. the alarm sounded off at 4.00 am & i silenced it quickly, of course, not wanting to wake sara. i have become a master at getting ready in near darkness. a half an hour later, i went off to work. these early dark mornings, i have to remind myself of where i have parked the car as i walked the rainy streets in front of the condo units. when i did drive to work i wondered what sara might have been dreaming about as i sleepily navigated.

by five am, i was in the baking mode as i prepped for breads & pastries to be utilized, or sold separately, during the morning & lunch meal periods. one by one, our small crew entered & started to work. we are beth anne, jackee, jonny, dan, & barbara & myself. we work, laugh, stress, & sometimes argue for a period of 8 to 10 hours each work day, during a stretch of an alternating five days for each one of us, out of six business days, each week.

feb 16<sup>th</sup>

it is the evening of the 16<sup>th</sup> & just before my very early bedtime. sara is out this particular night with friends & she has also been prone to disappear for occasional late afternoons or early evenings because of work-related commitments. i am at a lost without her tonight. because of our conflicting schedules, work schedule, & life schedule, it is unfortunate but we can go for days without interacting very much; however usually during a weekend we become in-synch again. but I do wonder, from her perspective, am i sometimes as lost to her?

as i review this day, in my mind, before bedtime i begin to become unfocused by drowsiness, but i do realize that there is nearly the same tone to this specific day as yesterday's day or as any other standard day in my recent life.

ok, maybe there was one exceptional incident from today but it did not occur at work. in the mid-afternoon, i was walking our feisty labrador, charly, & we bumped into one of our neighbors. she is a friendly chatty person, mrs. thornton, who has a reputation as the neighborhood gossip. it became a bit tortuous to have a conversational exchange with her while keeping charly reined in & while navigating the street during our walk & while thinking about my absent partner.

feb 17<sup>th</sup>

contentment is an ideal state of co-existence - but that state probably doesn't really exist or at least not consistently. i am not sure who said that. or maybe that unknown speaker was really talking about a concept such as thoughtful everyday living. so now i begin to wonder, as well, if any particular ideal state, of living, really exists.

for some mysterious reason i had slightly overslept thru the alarm in the early morning. sara climbed over me to turn it off & she playfully tousled with me until i was awake. she reminded me, at that moment, of someone that i would like to dream about. obviously, i am lucky to instead cohabitate with the real live person. anyway, she confirmed that i was really awake & she incandesced before she returned back to her own slumber.

despite the dreamy start to my day, work turned out to be more diverting than usual. jackee & myself were the first ones there & we were soon deep into our prep routine. we were uncharacteristically working alone, just the two of us, for the first 30 minutes or so. she told me a story of her childhood while we worked side by side.

"i was three, or three & a half years old, when i had my first realization of a jet plane." she said in wonder. "this was in baltimore, which is where i was born. and i saw the shiny object moving noisily across the sky." she smiled as she spoke. "i remembered asking my mom what the object was & she said that it was not a part of the sky but a type of large automobile that moved thru the sky. and since i was already familiar with cars & automobiles it seemed easy to think of it, the plane, as a new type of car." she smiled broadly as she continued.

feb 18<sup>th</sup>

i recall, as i am writing now, that i woke up in a panic in the early morning. sara was missing in action. i normally would crash much earlier than her but she was always sleeping soundlessly by my side when i awoke. i was ready to text her when i remembered. she had left me a note yesterday stating that she would be spending the night at her parents. charly looked at me knowingly, as i quickly readied myself for work. Hastily, i added in an abbreviated early morning trek, for charly, before going off to work.

i had hoped that jackee would have had the first shift again, at work this morning, but she didn't. instead jonny showed up first. lamentably, i had wanted for another one of jackee's stories. however, i did get a text from sara, at a rather inconvenient time during the morning rush. it was a cryptic, 'i owe you .. sorry, I've been m.i.a. lately', message. for a moment, I tried to mentally untangle her message, but unfortunately, i had to quickly return my attention to work. i actually worked the counter during the late morning & for lunch, which was a rarity. however, i must admit, that it was invigorating to interact directly with the customers.

i had a quiet thoughtful walk with charly, in the midafternoon, & i intentionally had to hide myself from our neighborhood's mrs. thornton. i had fortunately noticed her before she noticed me, she was also walking her petite dog & i shamefully ducked down another side street to order to evade her.

feb 19th

to my relief, sara was there, next to me, as the alarm went off in the morning. she was sound asleep & she had the faint aroma of thai on her breath & the faint scent of lavender on her body. just then, at that moment, somehow she seemed renewed to me or the same person only a little altered. charly ignored me, as i readied for work, he was quite aware of the party line, and that is, if sara is present, then she walked him in the morning & sometimes again at the noon hour.

to my relief, jackee was there, at work during the first hour. she offered another story. "i was about three years or so, of age." and of course, i thought it was interesting, at the time, that all of her stories occurred when she was three, but no matter. she continued. "my older brother challenged me to walk up a very large hill with him that was near our home. it was a lovely walk & an instructive walk, for my young self, but i was faced with a mystery when we topped the hill." she paused for effect. "there was another hill." she paused for effect. again. "when i asked my brother about this hill, he said that it was a just born baby hill belonging to the first hill. a fresh hill then & he announced with pleasure that we were probably the very first people to walk it." she continued her story in an animated manner.

to my dismay, charly was nowhere to be found when i returned home in my mid-afternoon from work. but i got a text soon thereafter. "if you are home by now, meet me & charly on the corner. and not the first corner but the second corner to the north." i exited the condo immediately & spied sara & our charly, who were both loafing on the second next corner. and as i approached i noticed that she had a name tag pasted over her shirt pocket that read, in all large capital letters, 'sara's iou.' but before i could just about reach her, she lip-synched, 'hurry up!' she was gesturing to the east which happened to be the present in-motion location of our indiscreet neighbor, mrs. thornton. and as i finally joined up with her & charly, we then hurried further on to the north.

the two midwest rivers that conjoin in the middle of country, the missouri river[1] and the mississippi river[2], are reported to meet in st. louis. Actually, this location is just north of st. louis in st. charles, missouri. technically the convergence, of the rivers, is a number of miles east of the city of st. charles near the village of portage des sioux.

traveling eastbound, on the missouri state road 94, from st. charles, will lead to the village & eventually to the lady of the river shrine[3]. the 20-foot statue, austere & assured, of the virgin mary, often referred to as the madonna of the mississippi, overlooks the mississippi river[4] & it is near the actual intersection with the missouri river[5]. at the shrine, one can observe the matured bluffs of illinois, on the other side. and regarding the rivers, at this location, one can witness clearly the severe conference between these vast bodies of water[6].

---

[1] the missouri river is the longest river in north america moving through the heart of the country. a river of earth & shadow.

[2] the mississippi river is a waterway of conveyance gracing minneapolis, st. paul, the quad cities, st. louis, memphis, baton rouge, & new orleans. a river of communication & light.

[3] the shrine is built in gratitude for the village's existence & continued survival within this tempestuous flood plain.

[4] the luminous illinois river also divests here, a few miles northwest.

[5] the worldly missouri river forcefully intercepts a few miles southeast of here.

[6] notably this co-mingling of rivers, the three, is akin to the large buoyant sound of an epic symphony.

---

   it is about three hours or so, the drive, from taos new mexico to gunnison colorado. in taos, the rio grande gorge[1] national scenic area abuts that city, in the high desert, dry & arid, and it is 800 feet at its deepest. it rambles about 75 miles. there are far vistas[2]. the colorings are pale green pale brown, the subtle grays[3].

   this compares favorably with the deep gorge[4] area of the black canyon of gunnison national park, which is near by striated roadway hill areas & near to the town of gunnison. this canyon is nearly 2800 feet, at its final depth, and about 50 miles in length & it can be crowded with evergreens & brush. here the mountains overshadow[5]. there are profound complexions here, dark green dark brown, the opaque grays[6].

---

[1] this is a deep earthen cleft with steep rocky walls
[2] these vistas have a sense of the timeless.
[3] those pigmentations pervade with a connotation of the aerial.
[4] this is a cavernous land depression with lofty stone walls
[5] these mountains have a sense of an infinity.
[6] those colorations permeate with a connotation of the primeval.

the quad cities[1], straddling illinois & iowa, are not four cities but rather five cities, that is, rock island, moline, & east moline in illinois and davenport & bettendorf in iowa. five bridges connect these cities over the mississippi river[2].

this is a region of industry; john deere headquarters, the rock island arsenal, & an emerging tech sector; and an area of higher education & cultural confidence; st. ambrose university, augustana college, & the putnam museum & the figge art museum. remarkably, in the quad cities, the flow of mississippi[3] changes temporarily from its customary north to south sequence to an east to west directive.

---

[1] once we walked an incandescent route on the river walk, in davenport, looking expectantly towards rock island

[2] once we crossed the sky bridge, in davenport, in its tinted glass tunnel, at sunrise, under a tilted sky

[3] once we took a water taxi, across a jubilant mississippi river, from moline to bettendorf

and then the green & russet towers of the glenwood springs canyon .. this follows after several miles, on interstate 70 west, from the white river national forest .. tightly, the windows in our car are closed up .. cool temperatures in the 40s .. and then the open prairies near the state border .. the city of grand junction, a land bound port into utah .. the temperatures have accelerated .. we are about to enter another state .. and then the great expanse of utah .. we indulge in the very first rest stop here .. these stops are far & few between .. it is higher than 100° .. loosely, the windows in our car are opened down .. it is a chalk & bronzed day .. and then the pivot near salina, route 89 north & route 28 north .. shadowed by the lanky servier bridge reservoir waterway .. here the waters are blue & white .. and then the juncture of interstate 15 north .. the ribbon thru the urban corridor of central utah .. that is, provo, salt lake city, ogden, & brigham .. we speculate about the great big great salt lake .. and then the idaho, this state of idaho .. the sun stumbles, it is nearer the 90s .. so now, now so - we perceive a light of an evening orange, a twilight red, & a nightfall purple – this is the light of repose & this is the light of restoration ..

the best tribe that we know of is our own .. as if in the middle of a vision, we are in the middle of the people .. a tribe is a constellation of people tied together by commonalities .. our ardent entreaty is that we save our selves from the oft-times small mentalities of our own stiff thinking .. to walk out into the field, with one's tribe, is to receive the gift of that place .. our earnest desire is to rescue our selves from the frequent psychic obstructions of static reasoning .. to lay down in the field, with the people, is an invitation to liberation & to those indulgences as offered freely by an unfiltered space ..

---

    ducks & geese wait in flooded fields .. in winter in the river valley .. we walk out of in to thru along those early morning lanes toward the wood & the water .. between there & here are small parcels of growing lands with agricultural housing .. the orange moon stubbornly abandons the sky .. in the valley with a river waits winter birds in engulfed fields .. water above trees is rain .. we are beginning to be beyond an edge of human domain .. the lemon sun overruns the sky .. the dirt below the trees is earth .. intemperate mallards ducks & the cold snow geese do not look directly at us, or do not nearly look near us .. the space between rain & earth is the natural world .. the wood & the water can barely *barely* acknowledge us ..

---

    It is difficult to distinguish between the actions of rising smoke, smolder, & steam .. the strident forms of noise produced by factories, are not unmusical .. the actions of low lying clouds, creeping fog, & the cold white matter of rain can be an amalgamation .. if we were to choose one day to savor, let it be today .. handsome atonalities are merely outside our generally accepted idea of harmonic substance .. the fortitude of now-ness, or the present moment, is the only one that we can really rely on .. the movable parts of the atmosphere & the engagements of industry could be an aggregation .. the blankets of freezing rain are a natural element that we might hold on to .. only one day at one time, that is today, can be held in our already ready hands ..

---

to begin with, you are alone when walking by the aromatic saturation of cultivated grounds .. this is a self-selected activity .. you experience the rich soil & it's wet botanic fragrances ..

near the other soaked commons, you quicken your walk but there are supplemental opaque infusions to contend with ..

it is solely the solitary you, the solitary humidity, & the dripping aromas .. you acknowledge, as well, the incrementation of a dense sun ..

freshly turned earth & newly made pools of green water; this has a familiar quality .. and you imbibe all of this with a sure stout stubborn conviction ..

---

absently, we consider the park, on a sunday, that is introverted inside this neighborhood near the college, which is soundless today - the inattentive academies .. it is not an abstraction, the park .. it has real flowers, blooms, & plantings that are laden with condensation that is composed of several textures & colorings .. we cannot help but notice a dripping corona in a pocket of the sky .. and we are aware that we might have borrowed someone's dog, of whom we know well, & this dog could be pulling us languidly by its leash as we move thru lush tunnels of gardens that are interrupted by land-defined depressions of naturally positioned ponds that are suitably augmented, around about anywhere, by slow moving small creatures & lethargic birds ..

we move across districts, thru zones,
in order to reach professional offices ..
our providers are housed in a nifty mid-century complex

it is one sprawling building with multiple levels & various accesses of entry ..
a smooth unbroken series of windowless monochrome rectangular annexes
except for the punctuation of generous portions of glass block

inside there is the anticipated modernist furnishings
and its appropriate period objects planted within a requisite spatial structuring;
this is seemingly a scene of a post-bauhaus balance between utility & the artistic

we look at the perfection of the pools of diffused light,
in various internal hallways, sourced from the bays of glass block,
that efficiently cohabitate with alternating currents of floating shadows

the construction of bridge structures, as in, an architectural fabrication that negotiates open space, or spatial obstacles, in order to connect to, or to provide passage between, two distinct & independent areas, often includes the utilization of falsework or formwork as part of the process ..

children imagine shapes & tools within their sports of play .. it is natural for them, thru games, and certainly in a parkland with a meandering though unpredictable stream, to want to bridge the distance between where they are & where they could be ..

falseworks are structural creations that provide temporary though necessary support during the creation of engineered spans within bridges .. formworks are temporary and/or permanent molds desirable for shaping concrete, & other relatable materials, that will allow for these poured materials to coalesce into a solid near-perpetual concretized form ..

children find logs, planks, or other forest materials to span the gap between two shores .. their temporary improvised solutions could often generate, & might regularly stimulate, a long-lasting developmental & beneficial pattern of cultural behavior ..

the northwest corner of 1$^{st}$ avenue, several blocks south of the west side of downtown, encompasses a sizable apartment building of 4 floors with a white plaster exterior & a medium brown triangular-styled roofline .. we would have wished that we might have resided there .. and then now this structure, with its design, is different from the other residences around it, apartments & some freestanding housing, which tends towards wood exteriors or brick externals with flatten rooftops .. on the interior, of this building, is an ample central hallway, but no elevator, and this interior features a fine foyer of marble & polished wood embellishments, with a noticeably elegant stainless steel-styled mailbox panel for the building residents & featuring two indicative comfortable doors that invite the residents upwards .. the upper floors, with aerial-styled hallways which have walls containing some wainscoting millwork, offer four large units per level & naturally, the units all, have excellent hardwood floors, classic bathrooms, mid-century room fixtures, & extremely enormous bay-styled windows .. of course, the first floor does inconspicuously conceal ground level spaces, such as quarters for the resident manager, the resident storage, the maintenance area, & the resident laundry .. we could have imagined that we may have lived there .. and then now this structure, with an added desirability, is convenient to the narrow green deep-styled park two blocks approximate & east ..

---

in oregon, a northwest state known for forests, there are countless tree farms ..
we do drive to one, it is a distance .. in the environment of the freshly scrubbed
air here, the exchanges within the atmosphere could be favorable .. the tree
farm, wooded land, is an area of managed growth .. we do walk thru one, for
some distance .. we are the native color of the woods .. rules of responsible forest
management are applicable here .. we are the rough-edged visage of the timbers ..
fast growing birch & pine, at times, are to be preferred .. in the environment of
the newly cleansed air here, the exchanges between us might be meaningful ..

---

.. a drizzled entreaty in routine city newsprint, a few arbitrary words .. because of this, we might think to consider the mountains .. mostly sunny, shifting barometries, with a trivial percentage of snow showers & ranging highs of 40 to 45 - after the noon, a caprice .. the blue southern blue mountains in the central highlands, an east wind up towards 5 mph slanting to the northwest, the north .. although .. more than that we could agree to ponder the coast .. partly sunny, uneven atmospherics, temperatures with a high near to 51°- before the evening, an elegy .. the bay at north bend, a regular wind ranging around near between about 8 to 19 miles tilting to the southeast, the south ..

we post hours,
on an obverse doorway ..
the newcomers advise doubt
but regulars walk in & might dialogue,
most sundays -
a mind, in honest motion, displays resilience ..

we position chairs
onto a correlative landscape ..
novices suggest uncertainty
though neighbors sit & may interrelate,
some saturdays -
a body, in earnest engagement, conveys confidence ..

after morning -
snowmass, colorado

on a self-conscious trail in the mountains
we know something about the mind of autumn
-- an inquisitive herd of yellow clouds follow us

a communal grove of highly polished aspens,
    one giant quivering organism,
        is housed in the retreating passion of an october

---

we fall upon a composing room,
with reproductive facilitators
& large format machines,
as we follow the lead of tradesmen ..

inside a typographer, in a language
of technical drawing & engineered design
of symbolic print & specialized papers,
speaks about today, as if it is a template for tomorrow ..

outside we encounter
light colored markings
up on or in side the dark mylar, the sky

we travel up several confident miles over iowa
and there is a level though comprehensive view ..
many circles of agriculture are laid
within the geometry of the land

we travel out only a few tentative feet beyond what is us
and accordingly, there is a fully realized albeit obtuse perceptive ..
several spheres of existence are positioned
inside the symmetry of the self

we are not lost, yet somehow though, we arrive to an unaccustomed place, perhaps north of the towns .. an ambiguous soundtrack swells in the background .. we notice extra people on the street, they seem buoyant .. we walk to a public house, a common establishment .. an uncertain lighting surrounds us which is similar to that of the provisional illumination frequently seen at recital halls before a much-anticipated, outwardly spontaneous, though thoroughly rehearsed, artistic performance .. the public house has doors, that we have found our way to, which are a transparent thick-plated glass with the words 'you are here' etched on them .. we notice ourselves on the street, we seem weightless .. and this public house has doors .. behind these, the one is waiting, & behind that one, the others are waiting ..

---

clouds/sleep/in/the/sea

a preoccupied sun
an absentminded river
are pictorial compositions
of negative space

but this is evident
or is it evidence (?)
an outside sky
which is forever
cleansing itself ..

the rains ends here
the rains begin here,
a terminus a boundary
a two-way aperture,
of inter-exchange

# CANTICLES

---

the inky calligraphic lettering of winter bare trees bare, in silhouette, observed while in automotive motion, in the unfolding hills, and as boosted by or backlit by a certain stream, a tilt, a mesmerizing slant, of brittle sunlight ..

our self(s) in the modest car
driving south on the highway,
below metro saint louis,
the missouri interstate-55,
handel's piano sonatas in the radio,
near an exit 143

———————————

then lightless altocumulus & stratocumulus -
certain formations of cloud pillars, some clouds,
which may well portend tentative beginnings

then limitless atmosphere -
the sky might be clearer, free,
as intended after a thunderous incidence(s)

eventually everyone passes thru here ..

a tiny village of less than 100, scattered about, which is essentially a rest stop, truck stop, travel center, motor inn, and rv park for the weary traveler .. at the junction of a national interstate and a prominent state route in the middle of a secluded region ..

a crossroads, a restless place of intermission - the winds & the dust may settle here, for the evening, but no one, no traveler, would dare remain here, for any extended length of time, because this is only a temporary stopover, a refueling or a revival service break, on the long journey to a somewhere else or to another distant place ..

---

we have just left the small village of madrid new mexico, a simple automobile ride, after consuming a cool water drink ..

then the route, state hwy 14, pivots up into the ortiz mountains .. then a trio of fleet-footed deer, mule deer, smoothly hops across the meandering two lane hwy onto the lands of a ranch, the lone mountain ranch .. then the descent into golden new mexico, a quaint hamlet, which is populated by only a few dozen people .. then a sudden uplift of the road again into the high airy country .. then a staggering lateral view of pyramids of mountain peaks; two bighorn sheep observe us from a perch on a high ground stony outcropping .. then a moment of blindness, or sightlessness, as we lose view of the road entirely, but momentarily, as we are distracted by the wide vista of yet another mountain range, covering a sheer third of the panorama, which is pitched at a respectable distance, suspended across a brunet rolling basin of enduring terrain ..

———————

a backlit congress of clouds
a little used forest road

    we stop to view a great rising of birds as they spread out from up above us .. their curvilinear trajectory is akin to moving coordinates enmeshed in an euclidean spatial system .. we are one point at one end of a diagonal line segment, a vector, between a here and a there .. we are as observers to a dispersal, an airborne scatter-chart of traveling birds, of elegant elliptic motion placed within a three-dimensional locus of land and of sky ..

---

leaving north odgen, utah, in the near dawn, we soon encounter the mountains when we connect to hwy 80 from hwy 84 .. the broad shoulders of the highlands continue well in to the state of wyoming .. the advancing dawn adds substance to the elevated contours .. in case of a strong tailwind, we chant tiny odes, declarations, or prayers from the pages of our agendas .. fiendish bursts of snowfall randomly impress as we journey east .. in case of a respectable delay, we intone little songs, entreaties, or canticles, from the linings of our journals .. we greet the modest cities, on these western highways, with intrigued speculation .. the burnished land spools on before us & on after us ..

_____

    we stir awake, and are alert, to a spectrum of distinct bands of visible brightnesses – sourced from above .. and is there a construct more uplifting than a skylight, an overhead roof window (?) .. and our boxy sleeping chamber is flush with new possibilities .. and the placements within this room – two steep wardrobe cabinets, in some corners, with seating in the other corners, as well as with a wide platform bed which is islanded in the middle - is now deliberate to our specific designing palate .. and that evident though ephemeral spectrum, a prism made possible thru the medium of our skylight, has become posted stationary above us .. and the continuum, of our existence, turns out to be possibly linked to a sort of, or it becomes akin to a kind of, voiced maybe knowable radiance ..

some people, we know, our neighbors, in our building, they are a bit older, have the rooms above us .. everyone has their particular taste in design schematics – who among us can truly gauge .. nevertheless, we do adore their sitting room .. that room has two moderately broad wide windows with lunettes, half-moon shaped glassworks, arched above them .. naturally, in the center of that room, are sofas, love seats, smooth chaise lounges, and dense leather chairs, all clustered together; and extremely large floor mirrors, leaning .. everyone has their unique opinion about objects and surfaces – who among us can truly comprehend .. but we sense that there is more at play here, in the sitting room .. perhaps a unseen field of implied depth or an invisible province of tacit dimensions ..

and so how with ease, we fall victim to the impossible cobalt of the sky, & the insistent sun, here in the southwest .. in particular, it is difficult not to notice the prevalence of chemtrails, chemical trails, or contrails, condensation trails, beyond us .. we are reminded that dramatic activity appear to be all around us ..

chemtrails which suggests unwholesome bio/chemical agents as disseminated into the atmosphere by unknown jet planes, have actually been dismissed by scientists as an erroneous assumption, while contrails appear to be factual and authentic ..

we wait on deep balconies, looking upwards, challenged by long thin skyward shapes .. to be precise, condensation trails, contrails, are mostly water-based streams, or water vapor, created in the air by high airborne planes, commercial or governmental, at upper altitudes .. we are aware of spontaneous movements which can be thought of as surrounding us ..

contrails which appear to languish and linger unwanted in our atmosphere, it has been noted, are innocently unpredictable as their rate of dissipation depends upon the prevailing atmospheric conditions .. and during their airborne tenure, contrails naturally spread out, in the higher regions of sky, into drawn-out narrow cirrus sheets or elongated cloud structures ..

x /

_____

we insert ourselves onto a pastoral grid .. and a line of winter trees are parallel to the road .. and a dark wooden telephone pole is at a ninety degree angle to the roadside .. and the attached telephone lines are perpendicular .. and black birds nesting, or inactive, on the telephone lines, are coordinate points, on an axis in a temporal coordinate system .. and we intersect the scene on a diagonal slope .. and we are likely positioned on state hwy 54, in southwest kansas, the state, as correlated between plains, kansas and meade, kansas ..

we are not novices in regards to the vagaries of life .. yet we travel to the far edges of the county, to the wind fields .. of course, wind, or vigorous breeze, is the bulk movement of atmospheric air – usually horizontal .. we, ourselves, take keen notice of mass events, obviously, as this phenomenon pushes us into the future .. wind farms, or wind parks, with its inherent wind fields, are a land/sky zone with a collection of towering wind turbines which are used for the generation of forthcoming energy ..

there is no accounting for the capriciousness of the life journey .. so then how incidentally, we are obliged to consult the authorities on the stable nature of wind fields and the instability of wind shear .. while a wind field is a broad region of some consistency of wind velocity, wind shear, on the other hand, is the sharp turbulence between wind speed and wind direction manifesting for a shorter duration of time over a smaller aerial/terrestrial region .. we weather the brief impulsive forces within our daily flowing daily constant hours as best we can .. we are apt to trim our beliefs, or possibly revise our tactics, in the face of such succinct capricious forces ..

in most octobers, the first half of those months, in the southern rockies, it is advisable to approach gingerly to the forests of autumn aspens, the golden cathedrals, in order to obtain a proper immersion .. it is a yellow world .. the smallish somewhat circular aspen leaves, turn from green to gold to rust before falling to the ground-soil and forming a thick carpet, thereby surrounding you on all sides - around and below, mesmeric, even before the sun enters into it .... likewise, the voices of the winds passing among the trees, an incidental whispering, and the pastel dome of the sky overhead augments it all .. it is a yellow & a blue world .. this is all surrounding you, felicitous, even before you enter into it ..

Who gives a voice to the voiceless wanderer (?), pondered a reporter, in San Diego, who is from a news organization.

She receives authorizations from the Homeland Department, travels to a few southwest detention centers, consults with security staff, interviews & video records asylum seekers, photographs within the detention facilities, and she discusses detention conditions with visiting charitable groups that offer support services.

Inside one such bleak facility, she photographs a makeshift poster, as drawn by a pale young man in a detainee jump suit; the poster features an expressive declaration and she hopes to use this declaration for the pictorial starter for her investigative article - este ascenso de una mala pesadilla, un infierno, solo para terminar en un limbo incierto, un purgatorio.

The reporter is, she is, bilingual, and in her mind she interprets - this ascent from a bad dream, a hell, only to land in an uncertain limbo, a purgatory.

Where might they house the fallen traveler (?), pondered a reporter from a news organization in San Diego.

She travels to Tijuana, consults with aid workers, is directed to provisional government facilities, and she garners details on the processes of locating and notifying distant relations; this process is facilitated through the examination of ID documentation and other belongings from a deceased migrant.

Outside one such unhappy facility, she photographs a wall mural which features a large sprawling proclamation and which she hopes to use for the visual intro to her news story - en el viaje a la luz, uno debe soportar las tierras oscuras..

She is, the reporter is, bilingual, and in her mind she translates - on the journey to light, one must endure the dark lands.

What might be the sentiments of permanent residents, of Mexico and the US, regarding immigration (?), pondered a reporter from a San Diego news organization.

She flies to Tucson and she purchases a one-way bus ticket on the Tufesa Bus Lines to Magdalena de Kino which is a quaint colonial city, in Sonora Mexico; $30 and a 3½ hours trek. And with her press ID lanyard in full display she talks to a variety of individuals of varying ethnicities and backgrounds in Tucson and Nogales, the US; she will speak to residents in Sonora during her brief residency in Mexico.

On the other side of the border, in Nogales Mexico, she departs the bus, with all passengers. She obtains a tourist card at the SAT Mexican Customs offices; the temporary visa is valid for seven days within the state of Sonora.

She notices, before she returns to her south-bound bus, a large sprawling mural on a nearby wall. She photographs the mural, actually it is a painted lettered statement, which features a commanding assertion and which she desires to use for the graphic opening to her newspaper piece - las únicas fronteras reales están en tu mente / abre tu mente.

The bilingual reporter, she, mentally deciphers – the only real borders are in your mind / liberate your mind.

He feels, Jason feels, that it is a waste of time to survey his closet because he essentially wears the same clothes, every week day, because of work; he wears Dickies' work pants and shirts, and hardy steel-toed work boots. He rents a room in a massive communal house in the Booth-Boyd district of Baltimore which is west of downtown; he works at one of the main postal distribution centers in downtown.

Jason's truck is similar to his week day clothing, that is, sturdy and reliable, and thoroughly practical.

Mail processing centers are cavernous places conspicuously skewed with noisy conveyors and sorting machinery. Mail handlers load and unload, wrap and unwrap, inspect and separate, and primarily, they perform all of this activity, and more, while standing or moving about.

Occasionally, Jason dons a certain portion of PPE, or personal protective equipment, as part of safety protocols, in specific designated zones of the processing floor. PPE could include work gloves, a reflective vest, safety boots, a hard hat, protective glasses, or ear plugs. Jason tends to work long overnight shifts of 10 to 12 hours which is obviously reliant on the particular postal season.

The days pass slowly and anonymously during his work week but if he is scheduled for two off days, consecutively, he leaves Baltimore City.

Destination - Gibson island, Maryland; which is actually not an island but a shapely strip of peninsular headland about an hour southeast of Baltimore City. Jason has, and he owns, a home, more of a work-in-progress than a finished house, which is located, in a modest area, just north, or perhaps, northwest of Gibson Island; Gibson Island is an upscale private island.

At home, near the Maryland coast, Jason wears carpenter's pants and a sweatshirt, and efficient tennis shoes, because he is constantly renovating, restoring, and updating his house, particularly during the intemperate times of the year.

If the weather is clear, and summer-like, he sails. He owns a catboat, that is, an eighteen-foot boat, single-hull, single mast, sailboat; christened *Vela Libre*. In truth, he co-owns the sailboat with married friends and close neighbors, Marsha and Jarrett.

On those mornings, when he can sail and enjoy the heroic currents of water and wind, in the Magothy River which flows into greater Chesapeake Bay, he wears pale canvas pants, a long sleeved t-shirt, a plain swim vest, a well-worn Orioles baseball cap, and carefree rubber-soled deck shoes.

'You have to meet her.' A friend of ours insists. We comply.

The friend had befriended this elderly woman, some time ago. She lives downtown, in our southwestern city, in an expansive collection of rooms.

We park in a public facility and we walk. The destination is surrounded, initially, by a high adobe wall, a typical rust brown stucco façade, which protects an ample internal brick-floor open patio. A smaller wall, not as high in height, is consequently encountered which protects a sharp and wide ascent of concrete stairs. At the top of the stairs, is her lodgings.

The unit is of a territorial style on the outside, with window frames etched in sky blue, and it features mid-century décor, and decorum, on the inside, all of which is carefully placed on handsomely maintained wide-plank wood floors.

Freddie, Alfred J Nordson, who is the friend, introduces us to Hattie, Harriet Beverly Anderson, who is the subdued serene senior woman; she seems to enjoy good reasonable health; she wears a long simple nuanced peasant dress which is draped by a stately wrap; she wears understated ballet flats. She wears only one single item of jewelry which is around her neck, a thick single strand of a silver necklace with an antique cameo attached to it; the latter dangling gracefully below her neckline.

Hattie moves with regal though aging slowness. She sports an elegant smile.

After introductions, and before Hattie's live-in assistant's attentions, a soothing woman named Alice, Alicia Luna Cena, who will eventually guide us to tea service, we are ushered into a singular room. The room has no furnishings but it does feature several tiny clerestory windows, on one side of the room, and near to the high ceiling.

Hattie speaks in measured cadences as she shows us laterally through an elongated photo gallery which is situated in the thin room and which presents vintage pictures, classic and crisp black/white photographs, duly annotated and dated - Hattie, family, and old friends. She offers a concise though visceral narrative, for each photograph, as we luxuriously view each one, in sequence.

In 1952, Hattie was of twenty years of age and apparently disposed to bouts of elegant laughter. She was prone to wear dark solid colored pencil skirts, or wiggle skirts, and lighter tinted long sleeve blouses with a ruffled neckline, and tasteful court pump shoes which featured confident, quite self-assured, four-inch heels.

# XVIII /

It is a leisurely drive south, from the nation's capital, on highway 95 and connecting on to highway 64, to the Hampton Roads Metropolitan Area[1] near the mouth of Chesapeake Bay; at a metro population of over 1.7 million citizens. The zone consist of nine independent cities – Hampton, Norfolk, & Virginia Beach among the most populated – which span seven counties in Virginia and North Carolina[1].

Perhaps, one might be most familiar with Norfolk because the city could be considered the central hub[2] of the metro area. The city abounds with richly revived historic neighborhoods and a vibrant cultural life – the Virginia Opera, Virginia Symphony, and Virginia Stage Company. And the city is home to the Naval Station Norfolk which is the largest naval base in the world.

A maritime and watery infrastructure[3] dominates the municipal setting, that is, bridges, tunnels, and docks, and rivers, lakes, creeks, canals, and other waterways. An abundance of parks, gardens, and green commons are evident throughout the city. The airport, Norfolk International Airport, in the north of the city, is surrounded, literally bounded, on three sides, by long lengthy waters and leafy green gardens.

---

[1] sometimes referred: the tidewater region as in the transient tides and sounds of low-lying coastal plains
[2] sometimes referred: the combined statistical metropolitan area as in the congregation of interrelated populous entities
[3] at times referred: a cultural heart as in a core humanizing character or spirit
[4] at times referred: an urban network as in the quintessential anatomic framework or underpinning

# XIX /

His first thought, Thomas Davidson's first thought, is about his umbrella as he drives out of his condo garage. Instead of the light mist which he had anticipated, there is a strong steady rain. He parks his car on the street, a truly short distance from his home, and he does a fast walk back to the condo. Before retrieving his umbrella, he blanks out for a moment but he swiftly recovers, before he exits, and then he walks back out into the street. As he is walking he has a sudden frightful realization that he has misplaced, or that he has forgotten, a recent segment of time.

Outside again, he is surprised that the rain has stopped and he winches slightly, he walks wobbly-footed, as he reacts to an on-surge of a sudden searing headache. Nevertheless, within seconds, he is standing next to what should be his automobile except that it is not his automobile; although this unknown car is quite similar to his own vehicle. Confused, he repositions himself in the middle of the street – it is a narrow hilly street; he lives south of the west side of downtown, Portland OR – and he looks around for his car while turning in a few unsteady concentric circles.

"Thomas. Hi. Do you need some help?" A woman, who suddenly appears and who is wearing a jogging suit & baseball cap, implores. Thomas responds with a look of non-recognition.

The woman speaks again. "Julie, actually Juliana Carson, we met earlier today. I just moved into the condo which is next to your unit." The unit, or units, is part of a collection of narrow, long, and tall rowhouse-type condos – garages on the first floor, steep stairs from the sidewalk which lead up to the living areas of the second and third floor; and drop-dead views, courtesy of a slim balcony, out of the back of the units; views, that is, views of the John's Landing, or the Macadams corridor; these neighborhoods are adjacent to the Willamette River.

"Apologies, but I don't remember us meeting before and right now I am looking for my car. I left it here, only a minute ago."

"Follow me." Julie suggests and Thomas follows her to the driveway which leads into his garage. "Your car in parked in your garage." Disbelieving, nonetheless, Thomas decides to check her supposition. He automatically presses his electronic car key and instantly a loud pert car horn beeps from within his garage; he has an American-made SUV.

Thomas, who has remained muddled, is about to speak but Julie holds up her hand. "Let me explain. As a preamble, I arrived late last night to my new unit and I had to use my sleeping bag because my furnishings would not arrive until today. This morning, at about 6.00 am, about 12 hours earlier than right now, I left my unit in order to jog down to the coffee shop, a few blocks away for coffee and a croissant. As I was leaving, I saw you walking towards your parked car and I witnessed you slipping on the wet streets and falling and then striking your head on the glassy strip next to the sidewalk. And .."

".. you approached, introduced yourself, and asked if I needed assistance." Thomas picks up the thread of the narrative. He presently has a light of recollection in the eyes.

"But you said: no, I am fine." Julie continues the thread. "And I suggested that you might want to consult a medical person – you see I am just beginning a new job, as a nurse, at the Oregon Health & Science University, OHSU – but you declined my suggestion."

Thomas continues, 'I remember getting into my car and returning it to my garage.' He takes a deep breath. "I went inside my condo, called my work to leave a message about my probable tardiness, took two aspirins, and I decided to lie down for a minute, or so, on the couch."

"I think you might have a concussion and your little nap turned into a session in which you passed out for hours. Your memory was probably foggy when you woke up." Harriet looks at Thomas carefully. "May I?" And she reaches up, with her hands, and she feels for a likely bump, on the sides and the back, of Thomas' head. He winces upon her touch of a particularly sensitive spot near to his right ear.

"So Thomas, may I now take you to the University hospital facilities? It is just up the hill, or hills, as you well know."

Thomas winches again as he clutches the side of head. "I think you are right, I do need to be checked out by doctor."

"Glad you agree."

Harriet retrieve her own car; she has a European-made SUV. They make small talk in the car on the way up into the hills to OHSU; incidentally, during the commute, they do discover that they are both single and unattached.

One person thinks, 'I hope we will become good neighbors.'

Another person thinks, 'I hope we will become a great couple.'

# XX /

---

"Where is breakfast?" Jaime de Lugo questions his wife, in Spanish[1], at an early hour on a Sunday morning in the city of Quito de Ecuador.

"There is no breakfast, at least, not for you, until the plumber shows up and fixes our shower. Correction, our showers. This is day three and the entire household has been inconvenience, don't you think?" Marta Celia de Lugo expresses serenely but firmly. "Remember our scheduled appointment with the plumber?"

"He missed Friday's appointment with us, right?" Marta Celia replies to her husband's question with a vigorous head nod which spurs Jaime to action. He marches to the master bedroom, retrieves his cellphone, and he calls the plumber, Servicios Plomería de Sergio. Sergio, of Sergio's Plumbing Services, is a master licensed plumber and as with all competent service professionals, in Quito, he is in high demand and he frequently/cavalierly overbooks his appointments; because he has the luxury to pick and choose.

Two minutes later .. "Where are you off to now?" She questions her husband as he has struggled into a light windbreaker and he has his car keys in hand.

"Left a message on Sergio's answering service and now I am off to find him. I know where he lives and I will go to his house."

"Remember how he missed another appointment, with us, two months ago but he did eventually make that one up. So, do you think you can bring him back, to the house, today?"

"I will try my best." Jaime presents his wife with a kiss and a hug and he is out the door. The de Lugo family reside in the well-regarded Barrio Bellavista, with its high streets, large protective walls, and overflowing though beautifully maintained gardens. Sergio's home is directly west, about a 10 to 15 minute commute[2], on the far side of Parque La Carolina.

Jaime parks on a charming and well-maintained street, disembarks from his automobile, and rings the buzzer embedded in the wall guarding the house and yard of the plumber and his family.

Soon, there is a quick clipped response, over a crackling speaker box, 'Who?'

Jaime identifies himself and greets the plumber's wife, Carla. Carla cheerfully replies and the gate buzzes. Jaime walks into the yard and he arrives to the front door. Carla is waiting for him. After more salutations and the appropriate face kisses, Carla immediately speaks up.

---

[1] all the ensuing references to conversations are realized as Spanish
[2] all the ensuing references to travel is realized as brief & picaresque

"Heard your message on the phone machine. So, my husband missed your appointment? You know he is one the best in the city and he is quite in demand." Carla explains with utmost sincerity and with more than a little pride. "But you and your family are a good customer and a friend." And she whispers, 'he is attending services at the wonderful old church[3], Iglesia de Santo Domingo. You know where it is located, I am sure, just 5 minutes or so, southwest of here."

"Yes, I am familiar with the location and it is indeed a beautiful structure. I will drive over there right now and many thanks, Carla."

"You're welcome. But, before you go, you must have a cup of fresh coffee and besides, the church services, at Santo Domingo, are only just beginning." As a social courtesy, Jaime indulges in coffee, and a tiny tasty slice of tres leches cake[4], and polite conversation, until he can reasonably excuse himself and finally depart for the old church. When he arrives, church services are still in progress, but instead of waiting outside, Jaime silently takes a seat in the very back of the well-preserved church and he turns his attention to the services; he discreetly does not partake in communion.

As the services conclude, the attendees solemnly file out of the church. It is Sergio who first notices Jaime and he waves in acknowledgement. Jaime joins the plumber, they pat each other on the back heartily, and they depart together.

"Alright, let me begin. I know that I missed your appointment and your showers are malfunctioning, correct. However, I did have a major emergency, I mean a really major plumbing job on Friday and Saturday. But I am available for you today. How does that sound?"

A startled though happy Jaime can only blurt out, 'yes, please. Yes. Yes.'

"Why don't we take my truck? You can leave your car here."

"Why would I leave my car here when we are going to my house?"

"Oh. I need to stop by a client's house for just a minute, or maybe five minutes, to change out some bathroom hardware. Don't worry, it will be quick."

Jaime agrees reluctantly and he joins Sergio in his truck. Fortunately, the client is only minutes south of their current location and nearer to the city center. And truly Sergio has only to replace faucet hardware in the master bathroom of his client; Sergio turns down refreshments, with deep contrition, as offered by the client, the Hernandez-Simas, during his service call. However, upon a rather quick completion of his task and upon his return to his automobile – Jaime is waiting in the truck – unpredictably, the plumber drives a few blocks further south.

"What are we doing in La Mariscal?" A confused Jaime offers. La Mariscal is a popular destination, near Quito Old Town and the downtown district, noted for its numerous restaurants, entertainment clubs, social hubs, and bars.

---

[3] all the ensuing references to oldness are realized as truly historic

[4] all the ensuing references to food & libations are realized as rich & delectable fare

"We must have breakfast. I do not think that you have eaten yet, am I right(?), and I know that I haven't."

Jaime could not argue with Sergio's logic since he was indeed quite famished. Upon arrival, they are fortunate to be seated promptly in the outdoor patio of a busy establishment, by an excessively gracious[5] hostess. They order breakfast and their waiter quickly returns with a basket of warm bread and with two pitchers of hot liquid, one of coffee and one of cream. He skillfully pour café con leches. Sergio phones his wife and firmly confirms that he is going directly to Jaime's house to work and that he will not be available for any other work assignments this Sunday.

While Sergio is phoning, Jaime decides to call Marta Celia; Jaime confirms with his wife that he has acquired the plumber.

"Then where are you, now?" Wonders Marta Celia.

Jaime explains that he and Sergio are at breakfast but that the plumber is firmly committed to his family's needs. Jaime's wife enquires about the name of the restaurant and then she advises her husband to bring home a box of pastries. 'They have an excellent bakery at that restaurant ..', she comments. Jaime pledges to bring home the requested baked goods.

Both men are off their respective cellphones when two sumptuous breakfast meals arrives. The waiter refills their coffee cups with warm café con leches. Within a scant few minutes, the hostess circulates through the patio area and upon approaching Jaime and Sergio, she politely enquires about their satisfaction with their morning meals.

It is then that Jaime realizes that he still needs to eventually retrieve his car and that probably Sergio will want to stop by his own home before continuing on to Jaime's house. And it is then that Jaime realizes he will be paying for two breakfasts, as a social consideration to Sergio, and that he would be expected to pay a Sunday/Holiday rate for the very kind plumbing services that he will be receiving sometime later on this same day.

---

[5] all the preceding references to courteous behavior are realized as a quintessential fabric of good society

Before Brett had an opportunity to meet Carlos, he was suspicious of him - because of rumors about him - but Carlos turned out to be his savior; Brett's savior, at least, initially.

Two years ago, Brett Johnson, a Canadian from Ottawa, arrived in Lima de Peru to begin his international teaching career, Upper School Mathematics, at the American School in Lima - Colegio Franklin Delano Roosevelt. His assigned school buddy, who was designated to help him with transition during those initial few months in Lima, Adan Santiago Neves, had recommended an apartment, in a zone near to the school, the San Luis district, which turned out to be a disaster - lots of unpleasant plumbing issues. Then Carlos, Carlos Bernardo Moreno, suddenly appeared in his life.

"You need a reliable apartment unit. I can help you." He suggested to Brett and Adan. A desperate Brett was persuaded despite his school buddy's reticence.

"El es un reparador." Adan cautioned.

"A fixer?" Brett queried. "Is that a bad thing?"

"Not necessarily. Just remember to be careful around him."

Brett ended up with a beautiful, albeit tiny, apartment in the upscale Miraflores area; only a few blocks from the Pacific Ocean. He was overjoyed despite having to pay a modest commission to Carlos and having to sign an intractable two-year lease and paying slightly higher than the standard monthly market rate for rent; it was much later that Brett discovered Carlos received a finder's fee from the management of the apartment complex.

o

While Brett remained friends with Adan, he tried to keep a distance from Carlos. A resourceful individual, Carlos worked part-time for the American school, as a teaching assistant, and he always seemed to maintain other outside odd jobs, enterprises, and projects within his career orbit.

Within one month, of Brett's initial arrival to Lima and as with any expatriate abroad, Brett tried to engage a weekly housekeeper but to no avail. Even Adan, who had helped with Brett's search, confidentially admitted, 'it is quite difficult to find someone who is reliable and who is trustworthy.' It is then that Carlos spontaneously joined him in the school cafeteria, one afternoon.

"¿Necesito una empleada? Puedo ayudarle" Carlos speculated.

And despite, his internal compass which suggested caution, Brett did engage Carlos to find him a proper empleada, a weekly maid. This turned out to be Carlotta; she cleaned his apartment and she would also run important and laborious errands for the Canadian whilst he worked, that is, grocery shopping, and the payment of utility bills and the payment of monthly rent at the appropriate service centers. In reality, Carlos had located a perfectly charming and efficient woman, who stayed loyal to Brett; Carlos did request a modest commission, from Brett, for his efforts. Of course, unknown to Brett, Carlos elicited a modest one-time gratuity from the maid.

o

Occasionally, over a period of two years, Brett would wonder about Carlos, 'is he really is a con artist? Or maybe he is just a smart business man? And how does he get his information?' He put these rhetorical questions to Adan on more than one occasion.

"He might be a bit of both." Adan elucidated sagely. "A con artist and an astute business man. As you know, it can be difficult making a living in South America, so it is understandable that a crafty individual, intend on surviving, would use creative means to achieve their desired ends. And in regards to how he is so knowable about literally everything? Essentially, he is an extremely good listener. A school campus, in particular, is a rife place for the spread of gossip and information." Adan sighed wisely, 'it is a good thing that you have mostly avoided his little overtures during your time here.'

o

Brett dated sporadically during his initial two years in Lima. Dating: a short-lived period, during year one, with another Canadian female teacher and a second short-lived period, during year two, with a Peruvian woman who was an employee of a local bank. As he signed a new contract, with the American school, for year three, he made a personal vow to establish a more substantive and lasting relationship with someone.

Mysteriously, Carlos found him one morning in his classroom, during a prep period at school. Brett was actually sitting at a student desk, instead of his own teacher's desk, laboriously grading student classwork.

"You know I think that you are one of the hardest working individuals here." Carlos announced as he unexpectedly waltzes into the classroom.

"I see about 140 students a day, so the paperwork is endless." Brett replied serenely after he had recovered from the abrupt entry of Carlos. "So, what's up?"

"You are looking for permanent girlfriend? Is that correct? A considerate, reliable, mature, pleasing, and intelligent person, yes?"

Of course, Brett was mystified because Carlos always seemed to have access to all manner of information about nearly everyone, or nearly every adult, on campus.

Carlos continued, 'I know someone who possesses those qualities and she desires those identical qualities in a life partner, as well. She is a single mother, with one child. She is Peruvian, educated, employed, and bilingual.'

A full minute of silence passed between the two men before Brett realized that Carlos had finished his pitch. Thoughtfully, Brett finally spoke up, 'Thanks, thank you, but no.'

Much to Brett's surprise, Carlos graciously nodded and offered a goodbye and he disappeared from the classroom. Brett returned to his classwork.

A few weeks later, Brett discussed the curious exchange with Adan. "I fully expected Carlos to continue to stealthy badger me over this set-up with this Peruvian woman but nothing; he has not approached me again about this scheme. And anytime we cross paths, at the school, we both exchange courteous salutations and then we both continue on our respective ways."

Adan and Brett were enjoying a pleasant coffee, on a Saturday, at a coffee shop near to Brett's apartment. "Perhaps, he has given up on his little enterprise or he has someone else in mind for this woman?" Adan shrugged his shoulder as he was speaking.

Brett nodded reluctantly.

Back at school, the following Monday, Brett collected papers from his faculty mail box. Among the papers was a letter which had been mailed from a local address. He was reading the letter, in his classroom, as students were filing into his first period Geometry class. As he finished the letter, with an astonished look on his countenance, he looked up only to find his students were staring at him and obviously waiting for him to start the class.

At lunch, that very day, Brett explained the contents of the letter to Adan. "The short version is that this woman paid Carlos, in advance, for three dates with me. Three dates which never occurred because I declined his offer from a few weeks past. Apparently, the woman's money is non-refundable."

"So, why is she writing you?"

"She is politely asking me if I would reconsider. She suggests having the three dates and then we could go our separate ways afterwards."

"And?"

"I think I will. After all, I would hate for the woman to lose her money. And I have a photo of her and her child. She seems nice. Take a look." Brett produced a photo which featured a poised woman who is holding the hand of a small child.

"She does look pleasant and trustworthy and intelligent. I guess it would not hurt to go out on a few dates with her but be aware that you will first have to seek out Carlos and inform him of your decision." Adan turned sardonic. "And expect to pay a some sort of commission fee to him; you know the drill."

A few days later, Brett walked several blocks south of the American school, to near the University of Lima campus. He met Erika Dolores Sanada at a small and extremely busy coffee shop; it served a variety of coffee(s) and pastries. She was behind the counter, working; she is the manager of the little establishment.

When Brett reached the counter, after waiting in the queue, Erika instantly recognized him "I am so sorry, Brett. You are Brett, right? Of course, you are." She was speaking competently in medium-speed English with a slight accent. "We are extremely busy right now and my other helpers called in, so I am alone. Can we reschedule?"

Brett was considerate of her circumstances but instead of leaving, he looked around at the crowded little café, and he decided to stay. "How can I help you?" He offered as he moved around the counter to join her. "Just tell me what to do." He said with an earnest smile. Erika gladly returned a smile as she passed Brett a clean service apron.

o

Within a week, Erika and Brett easily and pleasantly had moved pass the three-date threshold, as paid for by Erika. Brett also began to spend time occasionally at the café helping out Erika, or with Erika and her daughter, Edora, or with Erika and her family. Edora slowly warmed up to Brett over a period of time but especially after he introduced her to a Bilingual educational games/ activities app on his computer tablet.

Within a few weeks, Brett became thoroughly enchanted with Erika and her life, and the feelings appeared to be mutual on Erika's part.

Today: one month into their couple-hood, Erika and Brett and Edora are enjoying a sunny walk in a park just east of the American school, Parque Stella Maris. Brett has an epiphany. "Erika? Is Carlos still charging you? Obviously, we have engaged in more than three get-togethers?"

"No. Of course, not. Our agreement was for three dates only. Anything beyond that is our own private business and not his concern." She pauses and then she continues hesitantly. "Of course, there was a contingency to our arrangement and we might be obliged to him in the future."

Brett suddenly stops walking which prompts Erika and Edora to stop, as well. "Obliged?" He asks with great curiosity and with a touch of exasperation.

After a brief pause, Erika clarifies calmly, 'Yes, our little agreement guarantees him a bonus, should we be inclined to marry."

# INDEX

o u t l i e r
poems 2012-2019
© 2019

+++++++++++++

acknowledgments:
page 20 (quote) ode to the wave: pablo neruda: all the odes - Farrar, Straus and Giroux; Bilingual edition (July 2017)
page 22 (quote) ode to the present: pablo neruda: all the odes - Farrar, Straus and Giroux; Bilingual edition (July 2017)
page 23 (quote) ode to the book: pablo neruda: all the odes - Farrar, Straus and Giroux; Bilingual edition (July 2017)
page 32 (movie) another earth  - 2011 USA

page 33 (movie) pina  - 2011 Germany

+++++++++++++

thanks:
anne valley fox
james goetsch
jeannine kim
kim johnson
kristin walrod
madeline feijoo
theus

CPSIA information can be obtained
at www.ICGtesting.com
Printed in the USA
BVHW071012010419
544230BV00005B/485/P